Asian Noodles: 50 Delicious and Versatile Recipes

By: Kelly Johnson

Table of Contents

- Pad Thai
- Japanese Ramen
- Korean Japchae
- Chinese Dan Dan Noodles
- Thai Drunken Noodles
- Soba Noodles with Sesame Sauce
- Singaporean Laksa
- Vietnamese Pho
- Chinese Chow Mein
- Malaysian Char Kway Teow
- Taiwanese Beef Noodle Soup
- Indonesian Mie Goreng
- Burmese Shan Noodles
- Japanese Udon with Tempura
- Korean Jajangmyeon
- Thai Pad See Ew
- Filipino Pancit Canton
- Chinese Wonton Noodles
- Vietnamese Bun Bo Hue
- Japanese Yakisoba
- Malaysian Hokkien Mee
- Chinese Hot and Sour Noodles
- Thai Green Curry Noodles
- Korean Cold Noodles (Naengmyeon)
- Singaporean Hainanese Chicken Noodles
- Taiwanese Gua Bao Noodles
- Cambodian Kuy Teav
- Chinese Egg Noodles with Black Bean Sauce
- Japanese Noodle Salad
- Thai Coconut Curry Noodles
- Vietnamese Goi Cuon (Summer Rolls with Noodles)
- Malaysian Laksa Lemak
- Korean Spicy Cold Noodles (Bibim Guksu)
- Chinese Noodles with Garlic and Scallions
- Indian Chowmein

- Thai Sweet and Sour Noodles
- Japanese Tsukemen (Dipping Noodles)
- Chinese Stir-fried Noodles with Vegetables
- Taiwanese Noodles with Soy Sauce
- Vietnamese Noodle Salad with Grilled Pork
- Japanese Soba Noodle Soup
- Thai Peanut Noodles
- Chinese Braised Noodles
- Korean Banchan with Noodles
- Cambodian Noodles with Chicken and Lemongrass
- Chinese Spicy Peanut Noodles
- Japanese Zaru Soba
- Indonesian Soto Noodles
- Vietnamese Bánh Canh
- Chinese Pork and Noodle Soup

Pad Thai

Ingredients:

- 200g rice noodles
- 2 tablespoons vegetable oil
- 1/2 cup firm tofu, cubed
- 1/2 cup shrimp (optional)
- 2 cloves garlic, minced
- 1 egg, beaten
- 2 tablespoons tamarind paste
- 2 tablespoons fish sauce
- 1 tablespoon sugar
- 1 tablespoon lime juice
- 1/4 teaspoon chili powder (optional)
- 1/4 cup roasted peanuts, crushed
- Fresh cilantro, chopped
- Lime wedges, for garnish

Instructions:

1. Cook the rice noodles according to package instructions, then set aside.
2. Heat oil in a pan, sauté tofu and shrimp until cooked through, and set aside.
3. In the same pan, sauté garlic and beaten egg, then stir in tamarind paste, fish sauce, sugar, and lime juice.
4. Add cooked noodles and toss to combine. Adjust seasoning with chili powder, if desired.
5. Serve with crushed peanuts, cilantro, and lime wedges.

Japanese Ramen

Ingredients:

- 4 cups chicken broth
- 2 cups water
- 2 tablespoons soy sauce
- 1 tablespoon miso paste
- 1 tablespoon sesame oil
- 2 cloves garlic, minced
- 1 teaspoon ginger, grated
- 2 packs ramen noodles
- 2 soft-boiled eggs
- 1/4 cup green onions, chopped
- 1/2 cup cooked chicken or pork (optional)
- Nori (seaweed), for garnish

Instructions:

1. In a pot, combine chicken broth, water, soy sauce, miso paste, sesame oil, garlic, and ginger. Bring to a simmer.
2. Cook the ramen noodles separately according to package instructions and set aside.
3. Divide noodles between bowls and pour hot broth mixture over the top.
4. Add soft-boiled eggs, green onions, and meat (if using).
5. Garnish with nori and serve hot.

Korean Japchae

Ingredients:

- 200g sweet potato starch noodles (dangmyeon)
- 2 tablespoons sesame oil
- 1 onion, sliced
- 1 carrot, julienned
- 1 bell pepper, sliced
- 1/2 cup spinach, blanched
- 1/4 cup mushrooms, sliced
- 2 tablespoons soy sauce
- 1 tablespoon sugar
- 1 tablespoon sesame seeds
- 2 cloves garlic, minced
- 1 tablespoon rice vinegar

Instructions:

1. Cook the dangmyeon noodles according to the package directions, then rinse with cold water and drain.
2. Heat sesame oil in a pan and sauté garlic, onions, carrots, bell pepper, mushrooms, and spinach.
3. Add the cooked noodles, soy sauce, sugar, and rice vinegar, and stir-fry for another 2-3 minutes.
4. Sprinkle with sesame seeds and serve warm.

Chinese Dan Dan Noodles

Ingredients:

- 200g wheat noodles
- 1 tablespoon sesame oil
- 2 tablespoons soy sauce
- 1 tablespoon chili oil
- 1 tablespoon rice vinegar
- 1 teaspoon sugar
- 1/4 cup ground pork (optional)
- 2 tablespoons chopped peanuts
- Green onions, for garnish

Instructions:

1. Cook the noodles according to package instructions and set aside.
2. In a pan, sauté ground pork in sesame oil until browned.
3. Add soy sauce, chili oil, rice vinegar, and sugar. Stir to combine.
4. Toss the cooked noodles in the sauce mixture.
5. Garnish with chopped peanuts and green onions.

Thai Drunken Noodles (Pad Kee Mao)

Ingredients:

- 200g wide rice noodles
- 2 tablespoons vegetable oil
- 2 cloves garlic, minced
- 1/2 cup chicken or shrimp
- 1/2 bell pepper, sliced
- 1/4 cup Thai basil leaves
- 2 tablespoons soy sauce
- 1 tablespoon oyster sauce
- 1 tablespoon fish sauce
- 1 tablespoon sugar
- 1 tablespoon chili paste (optional)

Instructions:

1. Cook the rice noodles according to package instructions and set aside.
2. In a large pan, heat oil and sauté garlic, chicken (or shrimp), and bell pepper until cooked.
3. Add cooked noodles, soy sauce, oyster sauce, fish sauce, sugar, and chili paste (optional). Stir well.
4. Toss in fresh basil and cook for another 1-2 minutes.
5. Serve immediately.

Soba Noodles with Sesame Sauce

Ingredients:

- 200g soba noodles
- 2 tablespoons sesame paste
- 1 tablespoon soy sauce
- 1 tablespoon rice vinegar
- 1 teaspoon sugar
- 1 tablespoon sesame oil
- 1 tablespoon grated ginger
- 1 tablespoon green onions, chopped
- 1 teaspoon sesame seeds

Instructions:

1. Cook the soba noodles according to package instructions and rinse with cold water.
2. In a bowl, whisk together sesame paste, soy sauce, rice vinegar, sugar, sesame oil, and grated ginger.
3. Toss the noodles in the sesame sauce until well coated.
4. Garnish with green onions and sesame seeds.

Singaporean Laksa

Ingredients:

- 200g rice noodles
- 2 tablespoons red curry paste
- 1 can coconut milk
- 2 cups chicken broth
- 1 tablespoon fish sauce
- 1/2 cup cooked shrimp or chicken
- 2 boiled eggs, halved
- Fresh cilantro, for garnish

Instructions:

1. Cook the rice noodles and set aside.
2. In a pot, combine red curry paste, coconut milk, chicken broth, and fish sauce. Simmer for 10 minutes.
3. Divide cooked noodles into bowls and pour the hot broth over them.
4. Top with shrimp or chicken, boiled eggs, and cilantro.

Vietnamese Pho

Ingredients:

- 200g rice noodles
- 4 cups beef broth
- 1 star anise
- 1 cinnamon stick
- 2 cloves garlic, minced
- 1 onion, sliced
- 1 tablespoon fish sauce
- 1 tablespoon soy sauce
- 1/4 cup fresh cilantro
- 1 lime, cut into wedges
- Thai basil, for garnish

Instructions:

1. Cook rice noodles according to package instructions and set aside.
2. In a pot, combine beef broth, star anise, cinnamon stick, garlic, onion, fish sauce, and soy sauce. Simmer for 20 minutes.
3. Strain the broth and pour over cooked noodles.
4. Garnish with cilantro, lime wedges, and Thai basil.

Chinese Chow Mein

Ingredients:

- 200g chow mein noodles
- 2 tablespoons vegetable oil
- 1/2 cup sliced bell pepper
- 1/2 cup sliced onion
- 1/2 cup shredded cabbage
- 1/4 cup soy sauce
- 1 tablespoon oyster sauce
- 1 tablespoon sesame oil
- 1 teaspoon sugar

Instructions:

1. Cook chow mein noodles according to package instructions and set aside.
2. Heat oil in a pan and sauté bell pepper, onion, and cabbage until tender.
3. Add cooked noodles, soy sauce, oyster sauce, sesame oil, and sugar.
4. Stir-fry for 2-3 minutes and serve hot.

Malaysian Char Kway Teow

Ingredients:

- 200g flat rice noodles
- 2 tablespoons vegetable oil
- 100g prawns, peeled
- 2 eggs, beaten
- 2 cloves garlic, minced
- 1/2 cup Chinese sausage (lap Cheong), sliced
- 1/2 cup bean sprouts
- 1/4 cup chives, chopped
- 1 tablespoon soy sauce
- 1 tablespoon oyster sauce
- 1 tablespoon fish sauce
- 1 teaspoon sugar
- Chili paste (optional)

Instructions:

1. Heat oil in a wok and stir-fry garlic and Chinese sausage until fragrant.
2. Add prawns and cook until pink, then push to one side of the wok.
3. Add the beaten eggs and scramble until cooked, then add the noodles.
4. Stir in soy sauce, oyster sauce, fish sauce, and sugar. Toss in the bean sprouts and chives.
5. Cook until the noodles are slightly charred and serve hot with optional chili paste.

Taiwanese Beef Noodle Soup

Ingredients:

- 200g wheat noodles
- 500g beef shank or brisket, cut into chunks
- 4 cups beef broth
- 2 cloves garlic, minced
- 1 tablespoon ginger, sliced
- 2 tablespoons soy sauce
- 1 tablespoon rice wine
- 2 teaspoons sugar
- 1 star anise
- 1/4 cup green onions, chopped
- 1 tablespoon cilantro, chopped
- 1 boiled egg (optional)

Instructions:

1. Cook the noodles according to the package instructions and set aside.
2. In a pot, combine beef, broth, garlic, ginger, soy sauce, rice wine, sugar, and star anise. Simmer for 1-2 hours until beef is tender.
3. Ladle the soup into bowls with noodles, then top with beef and broth.
4. Garnish with green onions, cilantro, and a boiled egg if desired.

Indonesian Mie Goreng

Ingredients:

- 200g egg noodles
- 2 tablespoons vegetable oil
- 2 cloves garlic, minced
- 1/2 cup shredded chicken or shrimp
- 1/4 cup sliced cabbage
- 1/4 cup carrots, julienned
- 2 tablespoons sweet soy sauce (kecap manis)
- 1 tablespoon soy sauce
- 1 tablespoon oyster sauce
- 1/2 teaspoon chili paste (optional)
- 1 fried egg (optional)

Instructions:

1. Cook the noodles according to package instructions and set aside.
2. Heat oil in a wok and sauté garlic until fragrant. Add chicken or shrimp and cook through.
3. Add the cabbage, carrots, and stir-fry for 2-3 minutes.
4. Add cooked noodles, soy sauces, and chili paste, and toss until well coated.
5. Serve topped with a fried egg for an authentic touch.

Burmese Shan Noodles

Ingredients:

- 200g rice noodles
- 2 tablespoons vegetable oil
- 1/2 cup chicken, shredded
- 2 tablespoons soy sauce
- 1 tablespoon fish sauce
- 1 tablespoon chili oil
- 1/2 teaspoon turmeric
- 2 teaspoons garlic, minced
- 1/4 cup green onions, chopped
- 1 tablespoon roasted peanuts, crushed
- Fresh cilantro, for garnish

Instructions:

1. Cook rice noodles according to the package instructions and set aside.
2. In a pan, heat oil and sauté garlic until fragrant. Add chicken and cook through.
3. Stir in soy sauce, fish sauce, chili oil, and turmeric. Add the cooked noodles and toss to combine.
4. Serve topped with green onions, crushed peanuts, and cilantro.

Japanese Udon with Tempura

Ingredients:

- 200g udon noodles
- 4 cups dashi broth
- 2 tablespoons soy sauce
- 1 tablespoon mirin
- 1/2 cup tempura shrimp or vegetables
- 1 tablespoon green onions, chopped
- 1 sheet nori (seaweed), shredded

Instructions:

1. Cook udon noodles according to the package instructions and set aside.
2. In a pot, combine dashi broth, soy sauce, and mirin. Bring to a simmer.
3. Place cooked noodles in a bowl and pour hot broth over them.
4. Top with tempura, green onions, and shredded nori.

Korean Jajangmyeon

Ingredients:

- 200g wheat noodles
- 100g ground pork or beef
- 1/2 onion, chopped
- 1/2 zucchini, chopped
- 1/4 cup black bean paste (chunjang)
- 1 tablespoon soy sauce
- 1 tablespoon sugar
- 1 tablespoon sesame oil
- 1/2 cup water
- 1 tablespoon cornstarch (optional, to thicken)

Instructions:

1. Cook noodles according to package instructions and set aside.
2. In a pan, heat sesame oil and sauté pork, onion, and zucchini until cooked.
3. Stir in black bean paste, soy sauce, and sugar. Add water and simmer for 10 minutes.
4. (Optional) Mix cornstarch with water to thicken the sauce and add to the pan.
5. Serve noodles topped with the sauce mixture.

Thai Pad See Ew

Ingredients:

- 200g wide rice noodles
- 2 tablespoons vegetable oil
- 100g chicken or beef, thinly sliced
- 1 egg, beaten
- 1 cup broccoli or Chinese broccoli
- 2 tablespoons soy sauce
- 1 tablespoon oyster sauce
- 1 tablespoon dark soy sauce
- 1 teaspoon sugar
- 1/2 teaspoon vinegar

Instructions:

1. Cook rice noodles according to package instructions and set aside.
2. Heat oil in a pan and sauté chicken or beef until cooked.
3. Add broccoli, soy sauces, sugar, and vinegar. Stir-fry for 2-3 minutes.
4. Push ingredients to one side, add beaten egg to the pan, and scramble until cooked.
5. Toss everything together with noodles and serve hot.

Filipino Pancit Canton

Ingredients:

- 200g pancit canton noodles
- 1 tablespoon vegetable oil
- 1/2 cup shrimp, peeled
- 1/2 cup chicken, shredded
- 1/2 onion, chopped
- 1/4 cup carrots, julienned
- 1/2 cup cabbage, shredded
- 2 tablespoons soy sauce
- 1 tablespoon fish sauce
- 1/2 cup chicken broth
- 2 hard-boiled eggs, sliced (for garnish)

Instructions:

1. Cook the pancit canton noodles according to package instructions and set aside.
2. Heat oil in a pan and sauté onion, shrimp, and chicken until cooked.
3. Add carrots, cabbage, soy sauce, fish sauce, and chicken broth. Simmer for 2-3 minutes.
4. Add cooked noodles and toss until well combined.
5. Serve with hard-boiled egg slices on top.

Chinese Wonton Noodles

Ingredients:

- 200g egg noodles
- 10-12 wontons, cooked
- 4 cups chicken broth
- 1 tablespoon soy sauce
- 1 tablespoon sesame oil
- 2 cloves garlic, minced
- 1/4 cup green onions, chopped
- 1/2 teaspoon white pepper

Instructions:

1. Cook egg noodles according to package instructions and set aside.
2. In a pot, combine chicken broth, soy sauce, sesame oil, garlic, and pepper. Bring to a simmer.
3. Add cooked wontons to the broth and let them heat through.
4. Serve the broth and wontons over the noodles and garnish with green onions.

Vietnamese Bun Bo Hue

Ingredients:

- 200g rice noodles (Bánh Huế)
- 300g beef shank, sliced thin
- 200g pork, sliced thin
- 4 cups beef broth
- 2 tablespoons shrimp paste
- 1 tablespoon chili paste
- 2 stalks lemongrass, smashed
- 3-4 kaffir lime leaves
- 2 tablespoons fish sauce
- 1 tablespoon sugar
- 1/2 onion, chopped
- 1 tablespoon garlic, minced
- 1/4 cup cilantro, chopped
- Lime wedges and chili slices for garnish

Instructions:

1. Boil the beef broth, shrimp paste, chili paste, lemongrass, kaffir lime leaves, fish sauce, and sugar in a pot for about 30 minutes.
2. Add the beef and pork slices to the broth, simmer until tender, about 15-20 minutes.
3. Meanwhile, cook the rice noodles according to package instructions.
4. Serve the noodles in bowls, ladle the hot broth over the noodles, and top with cilantro, lime wedges, and chili slices.

Japanese Yakisoba

Ingredients:

- 200g yakisoba noodles
- 1 tablespoon vegetable oil
- 100g pork belly, thinly sliced
- 1/2 onion, thinly sliced
- 1/2 carrot, julienned
- 1/2 cup cabbage, shredded
- 2 tablespoons soy sauce
- 2 tablespoons Worcestershire sauce
- 1 tablespoon ketchup
- 1 teaspoon sugar
- A sprinkle of bonito flakes and pickled ginger for garnish

Instructions:

1. Cook the yakisoba noodles according to the package and set aside.
2. Heat oil in a pan and sauté the pork belly until browned. Add the onion, carrot, and cabbage and stir-fry for a few minutes until vegetables soften.
3. Stir in the soy sauce, Worcestershire sauce, ketchup, and sugar. Toss the cooked noodles in the sauce mixture until well coated.
4. Serve with bonito flakes and pickled ginger on top.

Malaysian Hokkien Mee

Ingredients:

- 200g yellow wheat noodles
- 150g prawns, peeled and deveined
- 100g pork belly, sliced thin
- 1 tablespoon vegetable oil
- 2 cloves garlic, minced
- 1/2 cup chicken stock
- 1 tablespoon soy sauce
- 1 tablespoon dark soy sauce
- 1 tablespoon oyster sauce
- 1 teaspoon sugar
- 1/2 cup chives, chopped

Instructions:

1. Cook the noodles according to package instructions and set aside.
2. Heat oil in a wok and stir-fry garlic and pork belly slices until browned. Add prawns and cook until pink.
3. Pour in chicken stock, soy sauces, oyster sauce, and sugar, then bring to a simmer for a couple of minutes.
4. Add the cooked noodles and toss everything together until well coated in the sauce.
5. Garnish with chives and serve hot.

Chinese Hot and Sour Noodles

Ingredients:

- 200g rice noodles
- 100g shiitake mushrooms, sliced
- 1/2 cup bamboo shoots, sliced
- 1/2 cup tofu, cubed
- 3 tablespoons soy sauce
- 1 tablespoon rice vinegar
- 1 tablespoon chili paste
- 2 teaspoons sesame oil
- 1 tablespoon garlic, minced
- 1/2 cup vegetable broth
- 1 tablespoon cornstarch (optional, for thickening)
- 1/2 teaspoon white pepper
- Green onions for garnish

Instructions:

1. Cook the rice noodles according to package instructions and set aside.
2. In a pan, heat sesame oil and sauté garlic until fragrant. Add mushrooms, bamboo shoots, and tofu, stir-fry for a couple of minutes.
3. Stir in soy sauce, rice vinegar, chili paste, and vegetable broth. Let the broth simmer for 5-7 minutes.
4. If desired, mix cornstarch with a little water and add to thicken the broth.
5. Serve the noodles topped with the hot and sour broth, garnish with white pepper and green onions.

Thai Green Curry Noodles

Ingredients:

- 200g rice noodles
- 2 tablespoons green curry paste
- 1 can (400ml) coconut milk
- 1 tablespoon fish sauce
- 1 tablespoon brown sugar
- 100g chicken breast, thinly sliced
- 1/2 cup bell pepper, thinly sliced
- 1/4 cup basil leaves
- 1 tablespoon lime juice

Instructions:

1. Cook rice noodles according to package instructions and set aside.
2. In a pan, sauté green curry paste until fragrant, then pour in coconut milk, fish sauce, and brown sugar. Simmer for 10 minutes.
3. Add the chicken slices and cook until done. Add bell peppers and simmer for an additional 5 minutes.
4. Add the cooked noodles to the pan, toss to coat them in the curry sauce.
5. Stir in lime juice and basil leaves before serving.

Korean Cold Noodles (Naengmyeon)

Ingredients:

- 200g buckwheat noodles
- 4 cups cold beef broth
- 1 tablespoon soy sauce
- 1 tablespoon vinegar
- 1 teaspoon sugar
- 1/2 cucumber, julienned
- 1 boiled egg, halved
- 1/2 pear, thinly sliced
- 1 tablespoon sesame seeds

Instructions:

1. Cook buckwheat noodles according to the package and rinse under cold water to cool.
2. In a bowl, mix cold beef broth with soy sauce, vinegar, and sugar. Chill the broth in the refrigerator.
3. Place cold noodles in a bowl, pour the chilled broth over them, and top with cucumber, pear, boiled egg, and sesame seeds.
4. Serve chilled as a refreshing summer dish.

Singaporean Hainanese Chicken Noodles

Ingredients:

- 200g egg noodles
- 1 whole chicken (about 1 kg)
- 4 cups chicken stock
- 3 cloves garlic, minced
- 1/2 cucumber, sliced
- 2 tablespoons soy sauce
- 1 tablespoon sesame oil
- Fresh cilantro for garnish
- Chili sauce for serving

Instructions:

1. Boil the whole chicken in chicken stock for about 45 minutes, then remove and set aside.
2. Cook the noodles according to the package instructions, then toss with soy sauce and sesame oil.
3. Serve the noodles topped with sliced chicken, cucumber, cilantro, and chili sauce.

Taiwanese Gua Bao Noodles

Ingredients:

- 200g wheat noodles
- 100g braised pork belly (Gua Bao style)
- 1 tablespoon soy sauce
- 1 tablespoon sugar
- 1 teaspoon rice vinegar
- 1/2 tablespoon hoisin sauce
- Fresh cilantro for garnish
- Crushed peanuts for garnish

Instructions:

1. Cook noodles according to package instructions and set aside.
2. In a pan, combine soy sauce, sugar, rice vinegar, and hoisin sauce, and simmer to create a thick glaze.
3. Toss the cooked noodles with the sauce.
4. Top with sliced braised pork belly, cilantro, and crushed peanuts.

Cambodian Kuy Teav

Ingredients:

- 200g rice noodles
- 100g beef or chicken, thinly sliced
- 1 tablespoon garlic, minced
- 2 tablespoons fish sauce
- 2 tablespoons soy sauce
- 1 tablespoon lime juice
- Fresh herbs (basil, cilantro, mint)
- Bean sprouts for garnish

Instructions:

1. Cook the rice noodles according to the package and set aside.
2. Sauté garlic in a pan until fragrant, add the sliced meat and cook until done.
3. Add fish sauce, soy sauce, and lime juice to the pan. Toss the cooked noodles with the sauce and meat.
4. Serve with fresh herbs and bean sprouts for garnish.

Chinese Egg Noodles with Black Bean Sauce

Ingredients:

- 200g Chinese egg noodles
- 2 tablespoons fermented black bean paste
- 1 tablespoon soy sauce
- 1 teaspoon sugar
- 1/2 teaspoon sesame oil
- 1/2 cup vegetable broth
- 1/2 cup bell pepper, sliced
- 1/4 cup green onions, chopped
- 1 tablespoon garlic, minced
- Fresh cilantro for garnish

Instructions:

1. Cook the egg noodles according to the package instructions and set aside.
2. In a pan, heat sesame oil and sauté garlic until fragrant. Add bell pepper and stir-fry for 2-3 minutes.
3. Add the black bean paste, soy sauce, sugar, and vegetable broth. Stir well and simmer for 5 minutes.
4. Toss the cooked noodles in the sauce, ensuring they are well coated.
5. Garnish with green onions and cilantro before serving.

Japanese Noodle Salad

Ingredients:

- 200g soba noodles
- 1/2 cucumber, julienned
- 1/2 carrot, julienned
- 1/4 cup edamame beans, cooked
- 2 tablespoons rice vinegar
- 1 tablespoon soy sauce
- 1 teaspoon sesame oil
- 1 teaspoon honey
- 1 tablespoon toasted sesame seeds
- 1 tablespoon green onions, chopped

Instructions:

1. Cook soba noodles according to package instructions, then rinse under cold water and set aside.
2. In a bowl, mix rice vinegar, soy sauce, sesame oil, and honey to create the dressing.
3. Toss the noodles with the cucumber, carrot, and edamame.
4. Drizzle the dressing over the salad and toss to combine.
5. Garnish with sesame seeds and green onions.

Thai Coconut Curry Noodles

Ingredients:

- 200g rice noodles
- 1 tablespoon red curry paste
- 1 can (400ml) coconut milk
- 1 tablespoon soy sauce
- 1 tablespoon lime juice
- 1 teaspoon brown sugar
- 100g chicken breast, thinly sliced
- 1/2 bell pepper, sliced
- 1 tablespoon fresh cilantro, chopped
- Lime wedges for garnish

Instructions:

1. Cook rice noodles according to package instructions and set aside.
2. In a pan, heat the red curry paste and sauté for 1-2 minutes. Add coconut milk, soy sauce, lime juice, and brown sugar, and bring to a simmer.
3. Add the chicken breast and bell pepper, cooking until the chicken is done and the sauce has thickened.
4. Toss the cooked noodles in the curry sauce.
5. Garnish with fresh cilantro and lime wedges before serving.

Vietnamese Goi Cuon (Summer Rolls with Noodles)

Ingredients:

- 100g rice noodles
- 10 rice paper wrappers
- 100g shrimp, cooked and halved
- 1/2 cucumber, julienned
- 1/4 cup fresh herbs (mint, cilantro, basil)
- 1/2 cup lettuce, shredded
- 1/4 cup carrots, julienned
- 1/4 cup hoisin sauce
- 1 tablespoon peanut butter

Instructions:

1. Cook the rice noodles according to package instructions and set aside.
2. Prepare the rice paper wrappers by soaking each one in warm water for 10-15 seconds until soft.
3. Lay the wrapper on a flat surface and add a small amount of noodles, shrimp, cucumber, herbs, lettuce, and carrots.
4. Roll the rice paper tightly, folding in the edges to create a sealed roll.
5. For the dipping sauce, combine hoisin sauce and peanut butter in a bowl, and serve with the summer rolls.

Malaysian Laksa Lemak

Ingredients:

- 200g rice noodles
- 1 can (400ml) coconut milk
- 2 tablespoons red curry paste
- 1 tablespoon fish sauce
- 1 tablespoon sugar
- 100g cooked shrimp, peeled
- 2 boiled eggs, halved
- 1/4 cup bean sprouts
- 1 tablespoon fresh cilantro, chopped
- Lime wedges for garnish

Instructions:

1. Cook the rice noodles according to package instructions and set aside.
2. In a pot, heat coconut milk and red curry paste, stirring until fragrant. Add fish sauce and sugar, and simmer for 10 minutes.
3. Add shrimp to the soup and cook until heated through.
4. Serve noodles in bowls, ladle the soup over the noodles, and garnish with boiled eggs, bean sprouts, cilantro, and lime wedges.

Korean Spicy Cold Noodles (Bibim Guksu)

Ingredients:

- 200g thin wheat noodles
- 1 tablespoon gochujang (Korean chili paste)
- 1 tablespoon soy sauce
- 1 tablespoon rice vinegar
- 1 teaspoon sesame oil
- 1 teaspoon sugar
- 1/2 cucumber, julienned
- 1 boiled egg, halved
- 1 tablespoon sesame seeds

Instructions:

1. Cook the wheat noodles according to package instructions and rinse under cold water.
2. In a bowl, combine gochujang, soy sauce, rice vinegar, sesame oil, and sugar to create the sauce.
3. Toss the noodles with the sauce until well coated.
4. Garnish with cucumber, boiled egg, and sesame seeds before serving.

Chinese Noodles with Garlic and Scallions

Ingredients:

- 200g Chinese egg noodles
- 2 tablespoons vegetable oil
- 3 cloves garlic, minced
- 1/4 cup scallions, chopped
- 2 tablespoons soy sauce
- 1 teaspoon sugar
- 1 tablespoon sesame oil

Instructions:

1. Cook egg noodles according to the package and set aside.
2. Heat vegetable oil in a pan and sauté garlic and scallions until fragrant.
3. Add soy sauce, sugar, and sesame oil, and simmer for 2 minutes.
4. Toss the cooked noodles in the garlic-scallion sauce and serve.

Indian Chowmein

Ingredients:

- 200g egg noodles
- 100g chicken breast, thinly sliced
- 1/2 onion, thinly sliced
- 1/2 bell pepper, sliced
- 1/4 cup carrots, julienned
- 1 tablespoon soy sauce
- 1 tablespoon vinegar
- 1 teaspoon garam masala
- 1 tablespoon oil
- 1 tablespoon fresh cilantro, chopped

Instructions:

1. Cook egg noodles according to package instructions and set aside.
2. In a pan, heat oil and sauté the chicken slices until browned. Add onion, bell pepper, and carrots, and stir-fry for a few minutes.
3. Stir in soy sauce, vinegar, and garam masala. Cook for another 2 minutes.
4. Toss the noodles in the stir-fried mixture and garnish with fresh cilantro.

Thai Sweet and Sour Noodles

Ingredients:

- 200g rice noodles
- 1 tablespoon soy sauce
- 1 tablespoon brown sugar
- 1 tablespoon rice vinegar
- 1 tablespoon lime juice
- 1/2 cucumber, julienned
- 1/4 cup bell pepper, sliced
- 1/4 cup fresh basil, chopped
- 1/4 cup peanuts, chopped

Instructions:

1. Cook rice noodles according to package instructions and set aside.
2. In a bowl, mix soy sauce, brown sugar, rice vinegar, and lime juice to make the sweet and sour sauce.
3. Toss the cooked noodles with the sauce, cucumber, and bell pepper.
4. Garnish with fresh basil and chopped peanuts before serving.

Japanese Tsukemen (Dipping Noodles)

Ingredients:

- 200g thick Japanese noodles (chilled)
- 1/4 cup soy sauce
- 1 tablespoon mirin
- 1 tablespoon sesame oil
- 1/4 cup chicken or vegetable broth
- 1 teaspoon rice vinegar
- 1 tablespoon brown sugar
- 1 boiled egg, halved
- 1 tablespoon chopped green onions
- 1/2 cup sliced pork or chicken (optional)
- Nori strips (seaweed) for garnish

Instructions:

1. Cook the noodles according to package instructions. Once cooked, rinse under cold water to chill and set aside.
2. In a saucepan, combine soy sauce, mirin, sesame oil, chicken broth, rice vinegar, and brown sugar. Simmer for 5-7 minutes to create the dipping sauce.
3. Arrange the noodles in bowls. Serve the dipping sauce on the side in small bowls.
4. Garnish the noodles with green onions, a boiled egg, and sliced pork or chicken.
5. To eat, dip the noodles into the sauce before taking a bite.

Chinese Stir-fried Noodles with Vegetables

Ingredients:

- 200g egg noodles
- 1 tablespoon vegetable oil
- 1/4 cup soy sauce
- 1 tablespoon hoisin sauce
- 1/2 teaspoon sesame oil
- 1/4 cup sliced carrots
- 1/2 cup bell peppers, sliced
- 1/2 cup cabbage, shredded
- 1/4 cup mushrooms, sliced
- 1/4 cup green onions, chopped
- 1 teaspoon ginger, minced
- 1 tablespoon garlic, minced

Instructions:

1. Cook the egg noodles according to package instructions and set aside.
2. In a wok or large pan, heat vegetable oil over medium-high heat. Add garlic and ginger, and sauté for a minute.
3. Add the carrots, bell peppers, cabbage, and mushrooms. Stir-fry until vegetables are tender.
4. Add the cooked noodles to the pan and stir in soy sauce, hoisin sauce, and sesame oil.
5. Toss the noodles and vegetables until well combined and heated through.
6. Garnish with green onions and serve immediately.

Taiwanese Noodles with Soy Sauce

Ingredients:

- 200g wheat noodles
- 2 tablespoons soy sauce
- 1 tablespoon dark soy sauce
- 1 tablespoon sugar
- 1/2 tablespoon rice vinegar
- 1 tablespoon sesame oil
- 1/4 cup sliced cucumber
- 1 tablespoon chopped green onions
- Chili flakes (optional)

Instructions:

1. Cook the wheat noodles according to package instructions and rinse under cold water to cool them.
2. In a bowl, combine soy sauce, dark soy sauce, sugar, rice vinegar, and sesame oil to make the dressing.
3. Toss the noodles in the dressing until well coated.
4. Garnish with sliced cucumber, green onions, and chili flakes (if desired).
5. Serve cold or at room temperature.

Vietnamese Noodle Salad with Grilled Pork

Ingredients:

- 200g rice noodles
- 150g pork (grilled or roasted)
- 1/4 cup cilantro, chopped
- 1/4 cup mint, chopped
- 1/4 cup basil, chopped
- 1/2 cucumber, julienned
- 1 carrot, julienned
- 1 tablespoon fish sauce
- 1 tablespoon sugar
- 1 tablespoon lime juice
- 1 tablespoon rice vinegar
- 1 garlic clove, minced
- Crushed peanuts for garnish

Instructions:

1. Cook the rice noodles according to package instructions and set aside to cool.
2. Grill or roast the pork and slice it thinly.
3. In a bowl, combine fish sauce, sugar, lime juice, rice vinegar, and minced garlic to make the dressing.
4. Toss the noodles with cucumber, carrot, and herbs (cilantro, mint, and basil).
5. Drizzle the dressing over the salad and top with grilled pork.
6. Garnish with crushed peanuts before serving.

Japanese Soba Noodle Soup

Ingredients:

- 200g soba noodles
- 3 cups dashi stock (or vegetable broth)
- 2 tablespoons soy sauce
- 1 tablespoon mirin
- 1/2 tablespoon sesame oil
- 1/4 cup green onions, chopped
- 1 boiled egg, halved
- 1 sheet nori (seaweed), cut into strips
- Optional: tempura or tofu for added texture

Instructions:

1. Cook the soba noodles according to package instructions, then rinse and set aside.
2. In a pot, combine dashi stock, soy sauce, mirin, and sesame oil. Bring to a boil, then lower the heat to simmer for 5 minutes.
3. Divide the cooked soba noodles into bowls and pour the hot broth over the noodles.
4. Garnish with green onions, a boiled egg, and nori strips.
5. Add tempura or tofu if desired.

Thai Peanut Noodles

Ingredients:

- 200g rice noodles
- 1/4 cup peanut butter
- 1 tablespoon soy sauce
- 1 tablespoon lime juice
- 1 tablespoon honey
- 1 teaspoon chili paste
- 1/2 cup carrots, julienned
- 1/4 cup cilantro, chopped
- 1 tablespoon chopped peanuts

Instructions:

1. Cook rice noodles according to package instructions and set aside.
2. In a bowl, whisk together peanut butter, soy sauce, lime juice, honey, and chili paste until smooth.
3. Toss the noodles with the peanut sauce until well coated.
4. Add the julienned carrots and chopped cilantro.
5. Garnish with chopped peanuts before serving.

Chinese Braised Noodles

Ingredients:

- 200g egg noodles
- 2 tablespoons soy sauce
- 1 tablespoon dark soy sauce
- 1 tablespoon sugar
- 1 tablespoon rice vinegar
- 1 teaspoon sesame oil
- 1/2 cup sliced mushrooms
- 1/4 cup bok choy
- 1/4 cup carrots, julienned
- 1/4 cup green onions, chopped

Instructions:

1. Cook the egg noodles according to package instructions and set aside.
2. In a pan, heat sesame oil and sauté mushrooms, bok choy, and carrots until tender.
3. Add soy sauce, dark soy sauce, sugar, and rice vinegar to the pan. Stir and simmer for 5 minutes.
4. Add the cooked noodles and toss to coat them in the sauce.
5. Garnish with green onions and serve.

Korean Banchan with Noodles

Ingredients:

- 200g buckwheat noodles
- 1 tablespoon soy sauce
- 1 tablespoon sesame oil
- 1 tablespoon rice vinegar
- 1 teaspoon sugar
- 1/4 cup kimchi (chopped)
- 1/4 cup pickled radish
- 1 tablespoon sesame seeds

Instructions:

1. Cook buckwheat noodles according to package instructions and set aside.
2. In a bowl, combine soy sauce, sesame oil, rice vinegar, and sugar to make the dressing.
3. Toss the noodles with the dressing and mix in chopped kimchi and pickled radish.
4. Garnish with sesame seeds before serving.

Cambodian Noodles with Chicken and Lemongrass

Ingredients:

- 200g rice noodles
- 1 tablespoon vegetable oil
- 200g chicken breast, thinly sliced
- 1 stalk lemongrass, finely chopped
- 2 cloves garlic, minced
- 1 tablespoon fish sauce
- 1 tablespoon sugar
- 1/2 cup cilantro, chopped
- 1 tablespoon lime juice
- 1/4 cup chopped peanuts

Instructions:

1. Cook rice noodles according to package instructions and set aside.
2. In a pan, heat vegetable oil and sauté garlic and lemongrass until fragrant.
3. Add chicken and cook until browned.
4. Stir in fish sauce, sugar, lime juice, and cilantro.
5. Toss the noodles with the chicken mixture.
6. Garnish with chopped peanuts and serve.

Chinese Spicy Peanut Noodles

Ingredients:

- 200g wheat noodles
- 1/4 cup peanut butter
- 2 tablespoons soy sauce
- 1 tablespoon rice vinegar
- 1 tablespoon sesame oil
- 1 teaspoon chili paste or chili oil
- 1/4 cup warm water (to thin the sauce)
- 1 tablespoon sugar
- 1/4 cup chopped green onions
- Crushed peanuts for garnish
- Optional: Sriracha for extra spice

Instructions:

1. Cook the wheat noodles according to package instructions, then rinse and set aside.
2. In a bowl, whisk together peanut butter, soy sauce, rice vinegar, sesame oil, chili paste, and sugar. Add warm water to thin the sauce to your desired consistency.
3. Toss the cooked noodles in the peanut sauce, making sure they are well-coated.
4. Garnish with chopped green onions and crushed peanuts.
5. For extra spice, drizzle with a bit of Sriracha before serving.

Japanese Zaru Soba

Ingredients:

- 200g soba noodles
- 1 tablespoon soy sauce
- 1 tablespoon mirin
- 1/2 tablespoon sugar
- 1/2 cup dashi broth (or water)
- 1 teaspoon sesame seeds (optional)
- 1/4 cup chopped green onions
- 1 boiled egg (optional)

Instructions:

1. Cook the soba noodles according to package instructions. Once done, rinse under cold water to stop the cooking process and drain.
2. In a bowl, mix soy sauce, mirin, sugar, and dashi broth to make the dipping sauce.
3. Serve the noodles on a plate or in a bowl, with the dipping sauce in a separate small bowl.
4. Garnish with sesame seeds and chopped green onions.
5. Optional: Add a boiled egg to the dish for extra flavor and texture.

Indonesian Soto Noodles

Ingredients:

- 200g egg noodles
- 1 tablespoon vegetable oil
- 200g chicken breast, thinly sliced
- 1 tablespoon ginger, minced
- 2 cloves garlic, minced
- 1 tablespoon turmeric powder
- 1 tablespoon soy sauce
- 1/2 cup coconut milk
- 1 liter chicken broth
- 1 boiled egg, halved
- 1/4 cup chopped cilantro
- 1/4 cup fried shallots for garnish
- Lime wedges for serving

Instructions:

1. Cook the egg noodles according to package instructions and set aside.
2. Heat vegetable oil in a pot and sauté the ginger, garlic, and turmeric powder until fragrant.
3. Add the chicken breast slices and cook until they are browned.
4. Pour in the chicken broth and bring it to a boil. Reduce heat and simmer for 10 minutes.
5. Add soy sauce and coconut milk to the pot, stirring to combine.
6. Place the cooked noodles into bowls and pour the soup over them.
7. Top with boiled egg halves, cilantro, fried shallots, and lime wedges.
8. Serve hot for a comforting and aromatic meal.

Vietnamese Bánh Canh

Ingredients:

- 200g bánh canh noodles (or thick rice noodles)
- 200g shrimp, peeled and deveined
- 1/2 tablespoon fish sauce
- 2 tablespoons lime juice
- 1 teaspoon sugar
- 1 tablespoon sesame oil
- 1 liter chicken or seafood broth
- 1/4 cup chopped green onions
- 1/4 cup cilantro, chopped
- 1/2 cup bean sprouts (optional)

Instructions:

1. Cook the bánh canh noodles according to package instructions, then set aside.
2. In a pot, bring the chicken or seafood broth to a boil. Add shrimp and cook until they turn pink.
3. Add fish sauce, lime juice, and sugar to the broth. Stir to combine and let the flavors meld for 5-7 minutes.
4. Pour the hot broth over the noodles in bowls.
5. Garnish with green onions, cilantro, and optional bean sprouts.
6. Serve immediately, enjoying the balance of savory and tangy flavors.

Chinese Pork and Noodle Soup

Ingredients:

- 200g egg noodles
- 200g pork tenderloin, thinly sliced
- 1 tablespoon vegetable oil
- 2 cloves garlic, minced
- 1 tablespoon ginger, minced
- 2 tablespoons soy sauce
- 1 tablespoon hoisin sauce
- 1 tablespoon rice vinegar
- 4 cups chicken broth
- 1/4 cup sliced mushrooms (shiitake or button)
- 1/4 cup bok choy, chopped
- 1 boiled egg, halved
- Chopped green onions for garnish

Instructions:

1. Cook the egg noodles according to package instructions and set aside.
2. In a pot, heat vegetable oil and sauté garlic and ginger until fragrant.
3. Add the pork slices and cook until browned.
4. Add soy sauce, hoisin sauce, rice vinegar, chicken broth, mushrooms, and bok choy. Bring to a boil, then reduce heat and simmer for 10-15 minutes.
5. Place the cooked noodles in bowls and pour the hot soup over the noodles.
6. Garnish with boiled egg halves and chopped green onions before serving.

www.ingramcontent.com/pod-product-compliance
Lightning Source LLC
LaVergne TN
LVHW081507060526
838201LV00056BA/2989